ALA Survey of Librarian Salaries 2001

Mary Jo Lynch, *Project Director*

ALA Survey Report

American Library Association
Office for Research and Statistics

American Library Association
Chicago and London 2001

ISBN 0-8389-8160-7

ISSN 0747-7201

Copyright © 2001 by the American Library Association.
All rights reserved except those which may be granted by Sections 107 and 108 of the Copyright Revision Act of 1976.

Printed in the United States of America.

Acknowledgments

Thanks are due to the many respondents who completed our questionnaires. Without their cooperation, this report would not be possible. We are grateful to the Association of Research Libraries (ARL) for sharing data with us as described in Appendix D and especially to Martha Kyrillidou, ARL Senior Program Officer for Statistics and Measurement, who sent the data electronically. We are also grateful to Ed Lakner, Diane LaBarbera, John Walder, Lidan Luo, Anita Michel, Andrea Brown, Amie Whittemore and other staff at the Library Research Center of the Graduate School of Library and Information Science at the University of Illinois who managed the mailings and processed the returns. Appendix A was prepared by Maxine Moore, Program Officer in ALA's Office for Human Resource Development and Recruitment. Finally, thanks are due to Julia Glynn, Administrative Assistant in the Office for Research and Statistics (ORS) for word processing the revised text and tables.

Table of Contents

Acknowledgments	iii
Introduction	1
Results	3
Director/Dean	4
Deputy/Associate/Assistant Directors	7
Department Heads/Coordinators/Senior Managers	10
Managers/Supervisors of Support Staff	13
Librarians who do not supervise	16
Beginning Librarians	19
Discussion	
Summary of Results	22
Salaries by Type of Position	22
Salaries by Type of Library	22
Salaries by Region of the U.S.	22
Problem with Categories New in 1999	23
Complicating Factors	23
Meaning of "Full-Time"	23
Meaning of "Professional"	23
Salaries Below $21,000	23
Job Levels or Faculty Ranks	24
Level of Experience	24
Appendixes	
A. Compensation Surveys Providing Information on Library Workers	25
B. ALA Policies Relating to Compensation Issues	32
C. Technical Considerations	36
D. Cover Letter	41
E. Survey Questionnaire	42
F. Salaries Paid for Less than a 12-month Year in Academic Libraries	47

Introduction

Librarians, the people who hire them, and interested others often ask the American Library Association (ALA) to tell them what salary might be paid to a librarian in a particular type of position, working in a particular type of library, in a particular part of the U.S. To fill the need for information of this kind, ALA began conducting a periodic survey of salaries for full-time professionals in academic and public libraries. Reports were published biennially from 1982 to 1988 and became annual in 1989.

This report, the seventeenth in a series, is similar to its predecessors in many ways but different in one important way which is described at the end of this Introduction. Otherwise, the 2001 report shares the following characteristics with its predecessors:

- It is based on salaries paid as of April 1st of the survey year.

- It is based on a survey of **libraries**, not individual librarians.

- It is based on a survey of **full-time** positions.

- It is based on a survey of **public and academic** libraries only. (Sources for salaries in other libraries are given in Appendix A.)

- It is based on a survey of libraries with at least **two professionals**. (See Appendix D for how this term is defined for public libraries and for academic libraries.)

- The public and academic library universe is stratified by the same **type/size criteria**: public libraries serving populations of from 25,000 to 99,999, public libraries serving populations of 100,000 or more, two-year colleges, four-year colleges, and universities. (The last category includes all institutions offering work beyond the bachelor's level).

- The nation is stratified into the same **geographic areas**: North Atlantic, Great Lakes and Plains, Southeast, West and Southwest (see Appendix D for list of states).

- It shows the **first quartile, median, and third quartile** for salaries paid in each type/size of library and region in addition to the **mean and range** (low and high) for each position reported.

- It shows salaries paid to staff **with master's degrees from programs in library and information studies accredited by ALA**.

- It shows salaries for **beginning librarians** in both public and academic libraries.

In the 1999 report, there was a change in how positions were described. Since the beginning, the ALA survey has collected salary data on staff holding three administrative positions (director, deputy/associate/assistant director, department/branch head) and three positions described in terms of content of work (reference/information librarian, cataloger/classifier, children's/young adult librarian). For 1999, the top two administrative positions remained and all other positions were collapsed into three, which focus on the nature of responsibility for the work of other staff: Department Heads/Coordinators/Senior Managers, Managers/Supervisors of Support Staff, and Librarians who do not supervise. This 2001 report used those same categories.

The changes were made for the following reasons:

1. The personnel systems in many libraries are not set up to provide the kind of information we were requesting (i.e., by position title related to job content).

2. Recent technological developments have led to the creation of many new positions in libraries. Although the titles are not standardized enough to warrant use in a survey instrument, without the salaries paid to staff in those positions, the results do not adequately represent the reality of the job market.

The Library Research Center of the University of Illinois Graduate School of Library and Information Science performed the mailing, processing, and computer analysis of the questionnaires. Mary Jo Lynch, Director of ALA's Office for Research and Statistics (ORS), directed the project and wrote this report.

We hope the results of the survey will be useful to employers of librarians who need this information in administering an equitable pay plan and to librarians seeking employment or career advancement.

Note: Since 1994, this annual salary survey has included unique "Supplementary Questions" which gathered information on an issue related to library personnel. For 2001, the questions were as follows:

1. What was your total payroll in the most recently completed fiscal year? Include salaries and wages for all staff. Do not include benefits.

    Total Payroll $ _____

2. Estimate your direct costs for staff development and training for all staff in the most recently completed fiscal year. This might include: expenditures for development and delivery of formal education events on site (e.g., speaker fees, materials), travel costs and registration fees for conferences, institutes, seminars, workshops, classes held off site, distance education, job related tuition reimbursement, purchase or rental of training materials (e.g., video, software), cost of a staff development office.

    Direct cost of staff development and training $ _____

Results will be published in late 2001 or early 2002 in *Library Personnel News* and will be posted on the ORS website (http://www.ala.org/alaorg/ors/reports.html).

Results

The survey questionnaire was mailed to 1,297 randomly selected libraries on April 12, 2001. Samples were drawn from twenty groups of libraries formed by stratifying five type-of-library categories by four regions of the U. S. Appendix D describes how groups were formed and sampled. By the end of June, usable responses had been received from 866 libraries, 66.8 percent of those sampled.

The results of this survey are presented on the following pages in six sets of tables. There are three pages of tables for each position. The first table presents salaries paid in medium-sized public libraries, i.e., those serving between 25,000 and 99,999. For each of four regions of the country and for the nation as a whole, the table shows the number of positions reported (N), the lowest salary and the highest salary (range), the mean (arithmetic average), the first quartile, median, and third quartile. This pattern is repeated for large public libraries (i.e., those serving populations of 100,000 or more), and for libraries in two-year colleges, four-year colleges, and in universities (i.e., institutions offering work beyond the baccalaureate degree).

The following example illustrates how to interpret the tables. In the first table for the position of director--the table presenting salaries paid in medium-sized public libraries--there were 82 salaries reported from the North Atlantic region. The lowest of these was $34,757 and the highest was $127,000. When all the salaries were added together and the result was divided by the total number (82) the average or mean was $69,386. When all the salaries were arrayed from low to high, 25 percent of them fell below $58,310, the first quartile, 50 percent fell below $67,964, the median, and 50 percent were above $67,964. Seventy-five percent fell below $79,813, the third quartile, and 25 percent were above that amount. The middle 50 percent of the salaries fell between $58,310 and $79,813.

Two caveats should be observed in reading the tables. The higher the number of cases (N), the more reliable the results of the sample in giving a true picture of the total population. When the number of cases is less than twenty-five, the results should be used with caution. This caution is especially applicable to the regional data for libraries where the number of professional staff is often small--medium sized public libraries, four-year colleges, and two-year colleges. Another caveat is that when the mean and the median are not close together, the mean is being influenced by some unusual values. When the mean is much higher than the median, there are several very high salaries. When the mean is much lower than the median, there are several very low salaries

DIRECTOR/DEAN
(Page 1 of 3)

Chief officer of the library or library system

Medium-sized Public Library
(Serving a population of from 25,000 to 99,999)

	Mean	First Quartile	Median	Third Quartile
North Atlantic N = 82 Range = $34,757 - $127,000	69,386	58,310	67,964	79,813
Great Lakes & Plains N = 84 Range = $33,372 - $115,000	69,130	55,614	69,426	79,298
Southeast N = 43 Range = $30,000 - $77,221	51,694	42,168	51,217	59,000
West & Southwest N = 52 Range = $37,943 - $109,432	65,151	50.261	63,870	74,637
All Regions N = 261 Range = $30,000 - $127,000	65,545	52,338	65,000	75,582

Large Public Library
(Serving a population of 100,000 or more)

	Mean	First Quartile	Median	Third Quartile
North Atlantic N = 30 Range = $61,099 - $205,993	101,224	78,900	88,907	119,020
Great Lakes & Plains N = 36 Range = $51,968 - $135,265	88,267	73,891	81,984	110,036
Southeast N = 40 Range = $45,000 - $119,980	82,340	65,088	82,323	101,413
West & Southwest N = 60 Range = $42,396 - $167,896	96,260	77,876	99,040	110,111
All Regions N = 166 Range = $42,396 - $205,993	92,069	73,946	86,729	109,143

Source: ALA Survey of Librarian Salaries, 2001

Director/Dean (Page 2 of 3)

Chief officer of the library or library system

Two-Year College

	Mean	First Quartile	Median	Third Quartile
North Atlantic N = 25 Range = $28,131 - $103,000	67,295	57,185	68,240	78,232
Great Lakes & Plains N = 28 Range = $37,000 - $82,100	56,108	45,830	54,885	64,007
Southeast N = 30 Range = $40,800 - $83,540	56,700	49,750	56,472	60,175
West & Southwest N = 23 Range = $37,000 - $73,182	57,860	51,000	59,976	66,083
All Regions N = 106 Range = $28,131 - $103,000	59,294	49,000	58,000	66,791

Four-Year College

	Mean	First Quartile	Median	Third Quartile
North Atlantic N = 22 Range = $32,000 - $115,000	67,971	53,249	58,582	90,000
Great Lakes & Plains N = 29 Range = $31,000 - $104,648	59,399	50,750	60,349	67,655
Southeast N = 20 Range = $31,000 - $90,643	48,978	35,250	49,839	56,786
West & Southwest N = 14 Range = $38,000 - $90,900	52,778	44,850	47,148	58,818
All Regions N = 85 Range = $31,000 - $115,000	58,075	45,871	55,000	67,150

Source: ALA Survey of Librarian Salaries, 2001

Director/Dean (Page 3 of 3)

Chief officer of the library or library system

University

	Mean	First Quartile	Median	Third Quartile
North Atlantic N = 51 Range = $42,220 - $168,000	77,247	55,811	71,185	96,773
Great Lakes & Plains N = 53 Range = $32,445 - $168,000	69,007	46,738	63,653	82,204
Southeast N = 49 Range = $36,780 - $160,000	81,759	58,248	78,189	98,200
West & Southwest N = 50 Range = $33,000 - $274,519	84,239	60,925	76,729	102,875
All Regions N = 203 Range = $32,445 - $274,519	77,907	55,455	71,000	95,256

All Academic and Public Libraries

	Mean	First Quartile	Median	Third Quartile
North Atlantic N = 210 Range = $28,131 - $205,993	75,446	57,797	70,245	86,781
Great Lakes & Plains N = 230 Range = $31,000 - $168,000	69,285	53,394	67,773	80,157
Southeast N = 182 Range = $30,000 - $160,000	67,051	49,980	59,979	80,984
West & Southwest N = 199 Range = $33,000 - $274,519	77,614	56,862	70,000	96,054
All Regions N = 821 Range = $28,131 - $274,519	72,384	54,509	67,746	85,000

Source: ALA Survey of Librarian Salaries, 2001

DEPUTY/ASSOCIATE/ASSISTANT DIRECTORS

Persons who report to the Director and manage major aspects of the library operation. (e.g., technical services, public services, collection development, systems/automation)

Medium-sized Public Library
(Serving a population of from 25,000 to 99,999)

	Mean	First Quartile	Median	Third Quartile
North Atlantic N = 65 Range = $26,250 - $109,000	54,720	43,747	52,163	63,885
Great Lakes & Plains N = 93 Range = $26,780 - $74,200	49,434	42,252	46,436	57,091
Southeast N = 44 Range = $28,000 - $56,000	40,032	33,445	39,029	46,022
West & Southwest N = 45 Range = $26,601 - $89,364	48,089	36,401	45,000	56,052
All Regions N = 247 Range = $26,250 - $109,000	48,905	39,377	46,297	56,052

Large Public Library
(Serving a population of 100,000 or more)

	Mean	First Quartile	Median	Third Quartile
North Atlantic N = 82 Range = $31,852 - $147,175	69,323	54,701	66,225	81,000
Great Lakes & Plains N = 92 Range = $36,608 - $119,882	67,577	54,573	61,400	79,696
Southeast N = 120 Range = $28,573 - $108,264	58,472	45,095	57,742	70,866
West & Southwest N = 139 Range = $26,520 - $115,003	72,133	58,941	73,752	85,738
All Regions N = 433 Range = $26,520 - $147,175	66,847	53,283	65,921	80,774

Source: ALA Survey of Librarian Salaries, 2001

Deputy/Associate/Assistant Directors (Page 2 of 3)

Persons who report to the Director and manage major aspects of the library operation. (e.g., technical services, public services, collection development, systems/automation)

Two-Year College

	Mean	First Quartile	Median	Third Quartile
North Atlantic N = 6 Range = $42,750 - $67,000	54,230	43,688	55,137	62,767
Great Lakes & Plains N = 13 Range = $29,489 - $55,000	40,060	34,372	35,556	47,237
Southeast N = 22 Range = $32,640 - $62,747	44,562	38,247	43,619	48,285
West & Southwest N = 16 Range = $31,000 - $69,911	48,382	37,297	46,005	58,714
All Regions N = 57 Range = $29,489 - $69,911	45,625	37,094	44,000	53,001

Four-Year College

	Mean	First Quartile	Median	Third Quartile
North Atlantic N = 18 Range = $29,814 - $78,529	49,981	36,760	50,987	60,834
Great Lakes & Plains N = 23 Range = $27,000 - $70,800	41,950	30,545	39,140	49,330
Southeast N = 13 Range = $25,000 - $52,210	34,137	28,000	30,000	41,646
West & Southwest N = 15 Range = $28,000 - $65,900	40,476	33,810	38,816	41,200
All Regions N = 69 Range = $25,000 - $78,529	42,253	31,091	39,140	50,987

Source: ALA Survey of Librarian Salaries, 2001

Deputy/Associate/Assistant Directors (Page 3 of 3)

Persons who report to the Director and manage major aspects of the library operation. (e.g., technical services, public services, collection development, systems/automation)

University

	Mean	First Quartile	Median	Third Quartile
North Atlantic N = 62 Range = $30,000 - $105,872	65,170	45,600	64,374	82,886
Great Lakes & Plains N = 57 Range = $25,000 - $101,014	60,657	40,199	62,586	79,954
Southeast N = 78 Range = $24,500 - $109,064	63,115	51,731	63,810	73,852
West & Southwest N = 107 Range = $26,000 - $200,000	64,602	47,775	61,789	73,536
All Regions N = 304 Range = $24,500 - $200,000	63,597	46,140	63,104	75,643

All Academic and Public Libraries

	Mean	First Quartile	Median	Third Quartile
North Atlantic N = 233 Range = $26,250 - $147,175	62,261	46,067	59,727	75,960
Great Lakes & Plains N = 278 Range = $25,000 - $119,882	56,682	42,652	54,148	66,581
Southeast N = 277 Range = $24,500 - $109,064	54,604	38,860	51,741	67,373
West & Southwest N = 322 Range = $26,000 - $200,000	63,616	46,709	62,920	77,652
All Regions N = 1,110 Range = $24,500 - $200,000	59,346	43,276	56,761	72,047

Source: ALA Survey of Librarian Salaries, 2001

DEPARTMENT HEADS/COORDINATORS/SENIOR MANAGERS

Persons who supervise one or more professional librarians.

Medium-sized Public Library
(Serving a population of from 25,000 to 99,999)

	Mean	First Quartile	Median	Third Quartile
North Atlantic N = 163 Range = $20,000 - $77,134	50,039	42,000	49,920	55,780
Great Lakes & Plains N = 164 Range = $22,545 - $67,787	44,608	37,311	44,591	50,914
Southeast N = 28 Range = $30,073 - $62,064	38,991	33,250	37,991	41,948
West & Southwest N = 76 Range = $27,113 - $82,140	50,194	40,762	48,991	61,177
All Regions N = 431 Range = $20,000 - $82,140	47,282	39,422	46,010	54,089

Large Public Library
(Serving a population of 100,000 or more)

	Mean	First Quartile	Median	Third Quartile
North Atlantic N = 477 Range = $32,503 - $107,187	55,421	49,800	55,303	61,000
Great Lakes & Plains N = 514 Range = $27,840 - $80,279	51,413	44,148	49,242	58,659
Southeast N = 402 Range = $24,000 - $79,752	48,993	40,909	48,927	55,381
West & Southwest N = 833 Range = $25,873 - $91,956	57,264	50,009	55,738	64,334
All Regions N = 2,226 Range = $24,000 - $107,187	54,024	47,150	53,227	60,791

Source: ALA Survey of Librarian Salaries, 2001

Department Heads/Coordinators/Senior Managers (Page 2 of 3)

Persons who supervise one or more professional librarians.

Two-Year College

	Mean	First Quartile	Median	Third Quartile
North Atlantic N = 15 Range = $38,563 - $74,000	57,378	47,581	60,000	68,000
Great Lakes & Plains N = 12 Range = $30,980 - $103,903	57,153	34,995	55,000	68,000
Southeast N = 12 Range = $33,000 - $78,182	47,454	38,097	46,400	53,983
West & Southwest N = 11 Range = $31,300 - $72,030	48,879	35,830	45,767	66,480
All Regions N = 50 Range = $30,980 - $103,903	53,072	40,493	50,964	67,658

Four-Year College

	Mean	First Quartile	Median	Third Quartile
North Atlantic N = 11 Range = $28,000 - $58,380	46,384	38,000	46,835	55,000
Great Lakes & Plains N = 10 Range = $31,070 - $69,680	48,137	39,103	46,500	56,810
Southeast N = 7 Range = $31,673 - $52,946	40,886	33,300	39,994	47,049
West & Southwest N = 4 Range = $37,100 - $54,400	43,025	37,325	40,301	51,450
All Regions N = 32 Range = $28,000 - $69,680	45,310	37,325	44,150	52,782

Source: ALA Survey of Librarian Salaries, 2001

Department Heads/Coordinators/Senior Managers (Page 3 of 3)

Persons who supervise one or more professional librarians.

University

	Mean	First Quartile	Median	Third Quartile
North Atlantic N = 66 Range = $32,000 - $109,253	50,812	40,647	46,363	56,495
Great Lakes & Plains N = 78 Range = $31,764 - $84,780	53,583	45,212	50,501	62,162
Southeast N = 105 Range = $31,454 - $75,900	50,445	43,355	48,978	56,908
West & Southwest N = 62 Range = $34,999 - $90,619	49,904	43,488	49,338	53,601
All Regions N = 311 Range = $31,454 - $109,253	51,202	43,300	48,750	57,303

All Academic and Public Libraries

	Mean	First Quartile	Median	Third Quartile
North Atlantic N = 732 Range = $20,000 - $109,253	53,711	47,637	51,697	60,188
Great Lakes & Plains N = 778 Range = $22,545 - $103,903	50,242	42,483	48,315	56,991
Southeast N = 554 Range = $24,000 - $79,752	48,627	40,373	48,131	55,035
West & Southwest N = 986 Range = $25,873 - $91,956	56,105	49,024	55,013	63,313
All Regions N = 3,050 Range = $20,000 - $109,253	52,677	45,000	51,482	59,930

Source: ALA Survey of Librarian Salaries, 2001

MANAGERS/SUPERVISORS OF SUPPORT STAFF
(Page 1 of 3)

Persons who supervise support staff in any part of the library but do not supervise professional librarians.

Medium-sized Public Library
(Serving a population of from 25,000 to 99,999)

	Mean	First Quartile	Median	Third Quartile
North Atlantic N = 153 Range = $22,984 - $75,344	44,073	36,850	42,210	51,497
Great Lakes & Plains N = 138 Range = $23,000 - $63,338	38,267	32,833	37,730	43,030
Southeast N = 49 Range = $25,773 - $73,560	37,333	31,144	35,400	42,955
West & Southwest N = 85 Range = $24,868 - $61,177	44,268	40,584	45,828	50,040
All Regions N = 425 Range = $22,984 - $75,344	41,450	34,379	40,986	47,000

Large Public Library
(Serving a population of 100,000 or more)

	Mean	First Quartile	Median	Third Quartile
North Atlantic N = 299 Range = $24,672 - $110,000	47,034	34,222	44,568	54,198
Great Lakes & Plains N = 179 Range = $27,330 - $70,489	43,779	37,741	42,507	47,616
Southeast N = 391 Range = $24,000 - $70,400	39,346	32,825	37,336	44,652
West & Southwest N = 742 Range = $24,480 - $81,276	41,822	35,292	40,510	47,380
All Regions N = 1,611 Range = $24,000 - $110,000	42,406	35,159	40,539	47,492

Source: ALA Survey of Librarian Salaries, 2001

Managers/Supervisors of support staff (Page 2 of 3)

Persons who supervise support staff in any part of the library but do not supervise professional librarians.

Two-Year College

	Mean	First Quartile	Median	Third Quartile
North Atlantic N = 23 Range = $29,696 - $71,667	50,080	42,000	46,097	58,000
Great Lakes & Plains N = 18 Range = $25,698 - $103,903	65,174	52,147	58,320	86,982
Southeast N = 22 Range = $30,000 - $78,830	45,717	34,903	45,422	53,385
West & Southwest N = 26 Range = $29,152 - $67,315	44,529	37,944	42,731	50,900
All Regions N = 89 Range = $25,698 - $103,903	50,432	39,250	49,197	56,150

Four-Year College

	Mean	First Quartile	Median	Third Quartile
North Atlantic N = 31 Range = $28,613 - $82,856	44,839	36,636	44,315	49,477
Great Lakes & Plains N = 45 Range = $29,500 - $63,550	40,912	34,400	38,162	47,450
Southeast N = 25 Range = $25,500 - $53,433	35,069	28,197	34,000	40,869
West & Southwest N = 25 Range = $23,900 - $51,979	36,019	32,100	34,722	39,430
All Regions N = 126 Range = $23,900 - $82,856	39,748	32,587	37,586	44,985

Source: ALA Survey of Librarian Salaries, 2001

Managers/Supervisors of support staff (Page 3 of 3)

Persons who supervise support staff in any part of the library but do not supervise professional librarians.

University

	Mean	First Quartile	Median	Third Quartile
North Atlantic N = 96 Range = $26,265 - $80,616	43,252	34,897	39,140	48,272
Great Lakes & Plains N = 132 Range = $24,000 - $77,681	46,465	37,945	44,457	53,640
Southeast N = 173 Range = $27,673 - $67,000	41,181	35,074	40,000	46,352
West & Southwest N = 120 Range = $27,000 - $87,804	44,418	36,823	43,396	49,893
All Regions N = 521 Range = $24,000 - $87,804	43,647	35,827	41,774	48,540

All Academic and Public Libraries

	Mean	First Quartile	Median	Third Quartile
North Atlantic N = 602 Range = $22,984 - $110,000	45,682	35,350	42,920	52,000
Great Lakes & Plains N = 512 Range = $23,000 - $103,903	43,486	35,951	41,519	48,596
Southeast N = 660 Range = $24,000 - $78,830	39,728	33,059	37,965	45,236
West & Southwest N = 998 Range = $23,900 - $87,804	42,267	35,292	41,521	47,380
All Regions N = 2,772 Range = $22,984 - $110,000	42,629	35,086	40,957	47,714

Source: ALA Survey of Librarian Salaries, 2001

LIBRARIANS WHO DO NOT SUPERVISE
(Page 1 of 3)

Full-time staff with master's degrees from programs in library and information studies accredited by ALA who were not reported earlier and who do not supervise.

Medium-sized Public Library
(Serving a population of from 25,000 to 99,999)

	Mean	First Quartile	Median	Third Quartile
North Atlantic N = 196 Range = $26,972 - $79,570	42,644	37,627	41,331	46,833
Great Lakes & Plains N = 273 Range = $21,425 - $65,000	37,826	33,507	37,294	41,596
Southeast N = 31 Range = $24,711 - $64,621	33,307	28,808	30,305	35,000
West & Southwest N = 106 Range = $26,062 - $58,344	41,858	34,488	42,540	50,337
All Regions N = 606 Range = $21,425 - $79,570	39,844	34,034	38,878	43,822

Large Public Library
(Serving a population of 100,000 or more)

	Mean	First Quartile	Median	Third Quartile
North Atlantic N = 922 Range = $25,324 - $85,632	41,144	34,561	40,566	43,500
Great Lakes & Plains N = 736 Range = $23,920 - $70,716	40,630	35,728	39,790	44,416
Southeast N = 386 Range = $24,136 - $59,350	36,262	31,291	34,116	39,423
West & Southwest N = 1,300 Range = $24,944 - $69,742	46,589	37,911	47,216	54,336
All Regions N = 3,344 Range = $23,920 - $85,632	42,584	35,569	41,309	48,555

Source: ALA Survey of Librarian Salaries, 2001

Librarians who do not supervise (Page 2 of 3)

Full-time staff with master's degrees from programs in library and information studies accredited by ALA who were not reported earlier and who do not supervise.

Two-Year College

	Mean	First Quartile	Median	Third Quartile
North Atlantic N = 27 Range = $27,560 - $100,000	58,817	35,795	56,000	87,000
Great Lakes & Plains N = 34 Range = $27,839 - $96,400	52,973	34,506	52,399	66,059
Southeast N = 33 Range = $27,000 - $82,326	43,850	34,969	39,420	48,313
West & Southwest N = 37 Range = $32,010 - $66,409	47,508	40,297	48,495	52,786
All Regions N = 131 Range = $27,000 - $100,000	50,336	36,507	47,858	59,765

Four-Year College

	Mean	First Quartile	Median	Third Quartile
North Atlantic N = 51 Range = $22,360 - $86,167	44,076	36,650	40,800	47,700
Great Lakes & Plains N = 32 Range = $30,180 - $62,267	42,547	37,830	40,217	45,376
Southeast N = 19 Range = $25,999 - $41,500	31,896	28,600	30,755	34,000
West & Southwest N = 15 Range = $23,900 - $69,220	39,747	32,267	37,058	45,098
All Regions N = 117 Range = $22,360 - $86,167	41,125	34,015	39,125	44,630

Source: ALA Survey of Librarian Salaries, 2001

Librarians who do not supervise (Page 3 of 3)

Full-time staff with master's degrees from programs in library and information studies accredited by ALA who were not reported earlier and who do not supervise.

University

	Mean	First Quartile	Median	Third Quartile
North Atlantic N = 254 Range = $24,000 - $100,094	47,693	38,257	44,765	53,673
Great Lakes & Plains N = 245 Range = $21,500 - $95,138	43,668	34,526	42,150	49,411
Southeast N = 290 Range = $24,500 - $68,700	39,445	34,000	38,538	44,040
West & Southwest N = 378 Range = $26,000 - $106,776	44,720	35,020	41,634	51,048
All Regions N = 1,167 Range = $21,500 - $106,776	43,836	35,272	41,301	49,125

All Academic and Public Libraries

	Mean	First Quartile	Median	Third Quartile
North Atlantic N = 1,450 Range = $22,360 - $100,094	42,926	35,351	41,501	46,527
Great Lakes & Plains N = 1,320 Range = $21,425 - $96,400	40,978	35,093	39,385	44,570
Southeast N = 759 Range = $24,136 - $82,326	37,567	31,836	35,894	42,000
West & Southwest N = 1,836 Range = $23,900 - $106,776	45,839	36,873	44,904	52,827
All Regions N = 5,365 Range = $21,425 - $106,776	42,704	35,340	40,895	48,114

Source: ALA Survey of Librarian Salaries, 2001

BEGINNING LIBRARIANS

Full-time staff with master's degrees from programs in library and information studies accredited by ALA but no professional experience after receiving the degree.

Medium-sized Public Library
(Serving a population of from 25,000 to 99,999)

	Mean	First Quartile	Median	Third Quartile
North Atlantic N = 15 Range = $25,000 - $42,025	34,061	30,275	33,200	39,000
Great Lakes & Plains N = 17 Range = $23,315 - $35,318	30,442	28,897	30,412	33,012
Southeast N = 9 Range = $21,071 - $37,423	28,678	27,212	27,800	30,444
West & Southwest N = 3 Range = $30,000 - $41,199	36,518		38,354	
All Regions N = 44 Range = $21,071 - $42,025	31,729	28,216	30,849	34,914

Large Public Library
(Serving a population of 100,000 or more)

	Mean	First Quartile	Median	Third Quartile
North Atlantic N = 87 Range = $31,267 - $42,508	32,507	31,296	31,296	32,176
Great Lakes & Plains N = 20 Range = $28,525 - $38,501	33,271	30,430	33,176	34,217
Southeast N = 59 Range = $24,000 - $37,442	30,370	29,712	29,985	32,067
West & Southwest N = 54 Range = $23,440 - $49,270	35,023	32,106	33,904	35,733
All Regions N = 220 Range = $23,440 - $49,270	32,621	31,296	31,633	33,618

Source: ALA Survey of Librarian Salaries, 2001

Beginning Librarians (Page 2 of 3)

Full-time staff with master's degrees from programs in library and information studies accredited by ALA but no professional experience after receiving the degree.

Two-Year College

	Mean	First Quartile	Median	Third Quartile
North Atlantic N = 6 Range = $34,700 - $48,109	40,335	36,575	40,000	43,527
Great Lakes & Plains N = 1 Range = $30,000	30,000	30,000	30,000	30,000
Southeast N = 3 Range = $30,000 - $44,487	34,996		30,500	
West & Southwest N = 2 Range = $42,000 - $44,000	43,000		43,000	
All Regions N = 12 Range = $30,000 - $48,109	38,583	31,550	40,000	43,500

Four-Year College

	Mean	First Quartile	Median	Third Quartile
North Atlantic N = 7 Range = $28,000 - $42,000	34,711	28,120	35,500	38,000
Great Lakes & Plains N = 9 Range = $28,000 - $40,199	31,873	28,000	32,000	33,330
Southeast N = 4 Range = $22,000 - $40,000	30,325	23,700	29,650	37,625
West & Southwest N = 2 Range = $28,000 - $30,000	29,000		29,000	
All Regions N = 22 Range = $22,000 - $42,000	32,234	28,000	32,000	35,625

Source: ALA Survey of Librarian Salaries, 2001

Beginning Librarians (Page 3 of 3)

Full-time staff with master's degrees from programs in library and information studies accredited by ALA but no professional experience after receiving the degree.

University

	Mean	First Quartile	Median	Third Quartile
North Atlantic N = 18 Range = $26,290 - $56,323	37,580	33,000	34,000	38,750
Great Lakes & Plains N = 16 Range = $28,000 - $45,600	35,635	32,250	34,879	40,000
Southeast N = 14 Range = $23,500 - $35,000	30,126	26,000	31,000	33,250
West & Southwest N = 23 Range = $22,000 - $42,000	31,458	29,500	30,600	34,500
All Regions N = 71 Range = $22,000 - $56,323	33,689	30,000	33,000	35,600

All Academic and Public Libraries

	Mean	First Quartile	Median	Third Quartile
North Atlantic N = 133 Range = $25,000 - $56,323	33,838	31,296	31,296	35,031
Great Lakes & Plains N = 63 Range = $23,315 - $45,600	32856	29,744	32,489	34,383
Southeast N = 89 Range = $21,071 - $44,487	30,314	28,150	30,000	32,067
West & Southwest N = 84 Range = $22,000 - $49,270	34,147	30,700	33,118	35,875
All Regions N = 369 Range = $21,071 - $56,323	32,891	30,145	31,918	34,361

Source: ALA Survey of Librarian Salaries, 2001

Discussion

Summary of Results

People interested in a particular type of library or a particular type of work, or a particular region will have their own way of drawing conclusions from the results of this survey. However, the results may be summarized in a very general way by noting that this survey included 13,487 salaries ranging from $20,000 to $274,519 with a mean of $47,852 and a median of $44,484. Another way to summarize is to look at mean salaries paid to particular types of positions, mean salaries paid by particular types of libraries, or mean salaries paid in particular parts of the U.S.

Salaries by Type of Position

The six positions are shown in rank order by mean of salaries paid on Table 1. Also shown is the mean of salaries paid in 2000, the dollar difference and the percent increase.

Table 1. Rank Order of Position Types by Mean of Salaries Paid

Title	2001 Salary	2000 Salary	Change Amount	Percent
Director	72,384	70,124	+2,260	3.2
Deputy/Associate/Assistant Directors	59,346	57,210	+2,136	3.7
Department Heads/Coordinators/Senior Managers	52,677	50,003	+2,674	5.3
Managers/Supervisors of Support Staff	42,629	41,224	+1,405	3.4
Librarians who do not supervise	42,704	40,838	+1,866	4.5
Beginning Librarians	32,891	32,160	+731	2.2

SOURCE: ALA SURVEY OF LIBRARIAN SALARIES, 2001

The percentage of increase in the mean of this year's 13,487 salaries over the mean of last year's 14,122 salaries is 3.75 percent. This figure is slightly lower than the increase in comparable occupations reported by the U.S. Bureau of Labor Statistics (BLS) in the "Employment Cost Index – March 2001" posted on the Web at: http://www.bls.gov/news.release/pdf/eci.pdf. That index increased 4.1 percent for the twelve months ending in March 2001.

Salaries by Type of Library

For the top two positions, Director/Dean and Deputy/Associate/Assistant Directors salaries were highest in large public libraries and lowest in four-year academic libraries. For the other four categories, salaries were usually highest in two-year academic libraries and lowest in four-year college libraries.

Salaries by Region of the U.S.

In order to determine which region has the highest salaries, we analyzed the six positions and the five library size/type categories. When the region with the highest mean salary was marked for each position in each size/type category, North Atlantic was checked 63 percent of the time and West and Southwest was highest 26 percent of the time. Great Lakes and Plains was highest three times. This pattern is a change from last year when West and Southwest was highest 40 percent of the time and North Atlantic was highest 43 percent of the time. The lowest mean salary was in the Southeast 73 percent of the time. Great Lakes and Plains was lowest five times, and West and Southwest was lowest three times. North Atlantic was never lowest and Southeast was never highest.

Problem with Categories New in 1999

There is one problem with the above summary paragraphs, stemming from changes made in the questionnaire in 1999. For libraries in the Association of Research Libraries (ARL), we did not have salaries in two categories: Department Heads/Coordinators/Senior Managers and Managers/Supervisors of Support Staff. We use data already collected by ARL for ARL libraries in our sample, and ARL does not use those two categories. Therefore we knew we do not have salaries in those categories for the 22 ARL libraries in our sample this year.

Complicating Factors

When designing this survey in the early 1980s, we were aware that several aspects of the patterns of employment in libraries would complicate our efforts. As we talked with respondents and users of the reports over the years, we gained additional insights into several factors which should be taken into consideration when using these results.

The Meaning of "Full-Time"

The questionnaire asked about salaries for **full-time** positions only, but full-time was not defined. There are at least two problems in this area: How many months in a year is full-time? How do you report people who work full-time in the library but part-time at one job and part-time at another?

The months in a year problem primarily affects academic libraries where librarians sometimes have academic year contracts for less than twelve months. In this survey, respondents are asked to indicate the number of months a salary covers and the computer calculated twelve months at the same rate. Appendix G shows how often less-than-twelve-month salaries occur.

The Meaning of "Professional"

In the early years of this survey, respondents were asked to report only salaries paid to professionals, but the word "professional" was not defined. Instead, each position was described in such a way that professional responsibility was clearly implied. Instructions told the respondent to list all incumbents in these positions "regardless of academic credentials." We accepted the judgement of the respondent that the salaries reported were for professional work but found out, when we called about low salaries (see below) that some respondents had doubts about whether a particular incumbent could be described as "professional." When such doubts were expressed, we asked the respondent to make a decision based on the definition in ALA's statement on "Library Education and Personnel Utilization." (See Appendix B, Policy 54.1, Section 8) In 1990, that definition was added to the instructions. Beginning with the 1991 survey, we asked respondents to report only staff *with master's degrees from programs in library and information studies accredited by ALA*.

Salaries Below $22,000

In previous years, this report has described the methodology used to determine the cut-off point below which salaries were investigated as probably not being full-time, professional work. The cut-off for the 2001 survey was $22,000. Of the 13,508 salaries initially considered usable, 28 were below $22,000 (less than 1%). Staff at the Library Research Center used e-mail or telephone to contact the person named as the respondent at the 18 libraries involved. They learned that 21 salaries were for part-time work, were for non-professional positions, or were filled out in error. Those 21 salaries were dropped from the data file used for this report. The dropped salaries had been reported primarily because the respondent had misunderstood the instructions. Once the salaries were dropped, the total usable number of salaries was 13,487. Seven salaries of less than $22,000 did remain in the file. Of these, two salaries were in academic libraries and five were in public libraries.

Job Levels or Faculty Ranks

The wording of this questionnaire is based on an assumption that librarians are compensated at a particular amount for assuming a particular level of responsibility. However, in many libraries that is not true. Some libraries use a system of levels in their compensation structure (e.g., Librarian I, II, III, IV) to account for the background a person brings to a job and the amount of experience the person has. Some academic libraries pay salaries based on faculty rank rather than work done. In many academic libraries where librarians have faculty rank and titles, they are compensated as Instructor, Assistant Professor, Associate Professor or Professor and not as any one of the position categories on our questionnaire. We do not attempt to account for this variety within the structure of our questionnaire.

Several respondents and reviewers of this report have recommended in the past that we collect salary data for librarian levels or ranks. We have considered this seriously, but concluded that it would be at least as confusing as the current method due to the fact that levels and ranks mean different things in different libraries.

Level of Experience

Respondents occasionally ask us to ask for and report salaries in a way that takes into account the years of experience that an incumbent possesses. Unfortunately, providing that information would be a burden on respondents and reporting it would make this report overly complex. This report does take such factors into account in two ways: beginning librarians are reported in a separate table and are not included in salary data for other positions; and data for all positions show figures at the first and third quartile as well as the mean, median, and range.

Appendix A

Compensation Surveys Providing Information on Library Workers

Most library salary surveys listed below are conducted on a regular schedule (annual or biennial) and on a regional or national basis. The library literature should be monitored for reports of one-time surveys by individual libraries or associations. Some state library agencies collect salary and benefits data as part of their ongoing statistical gathering efforts from libraries within their own state. There is wide variation, however, in what data are collected and how these are compiled and reported. Most collect only public library data. Academic and school library data may be collected by other state agencies.

In addition, some state library associations collect salary data, issue recommended salary guidelines, set minimum salaries for professional positions, or publish reports in association journals or newsletters. As of August 2001, nineteen states had established recommended minimum salaries. These include: Connecticut, Delaware, Illinois, Indiana, Iowa, Louisiana, Maine, Massachusetts, New Jersey, North Carolina, Ohio, Pennsylvania, Rhode Island, South Carolina, South Dakota, Texas, Vermont, West Virginia, and Wisconsin. Specific amounts are not listed here because these are updated regularly by the associations. The latest figures can be found in the most recent classified section of *American Libraries* or *College & Research Libraries News*. A list of state library agency and association addresses can be found in *The Bowker Annual: Library and Book Trade Almanac*.

Individual libraries will sometimes conduct private surveys of institutions of comparable size or in the same geographical area, either through an outside consulting firm or by calling libraries informally. For the most part, these surveys are not published, although the initiating library will often share results with participating libraries. Some library workers are also conducting surveys that compare their salaries with other professions and occupations within their jurisdiction in an effort to achieve pay equity with positions requiring comparable skills, effort, responsibilities and working conditions.

Academic Libraries

Association of Research Libraries. *ARL Annual Salary Survey*. Washington, D.C.: ARL, 1973-.

> The 2000-01 compilation consists of detailed tables of salaries for over 12,000 professional positions based on data collected from ARL member libraries and analyzed by job category, years of experience, sex, minority status, size of library, and geographic region. Included in the publication are tables for general, medical, law, Canadian libraries and non-university research libraries. Information on this and other ARL products and services can be found at www.arl.org.

> To order, contact ARL Publications Distribution Center, PO Box 531, Annapolis Junction, MD 20701-0531, 301/362-8196, fax 301/206-9789, pubs@arl.org. This survey is available for

$44/ARL members or $100/nonmembers, plus $6 s/h per publication.

College and University Professional Association for Human Resources. 2000-*01 Administrative Compensation Survey*. Washington, D.C.: CUPA-HR.

The survey includes data on 167 college and university administrative positions from 1,466 public and private institutions. The tables in the survey present the median salary according to institutional budget, enrollment, and classification. Directors of library services are included.

The survey is available from CUPA-HR, 1233 20th St., NW, Suite 301, Washington, D.C. 20035-1250, 202/429-0311, fax 202/429-0149, www.cupahr.org; $100 for association members/survey participants, $165 for members/non-participants, $195 for non-members/survey participants and $330 for nonmembers/survey non-participants.

College and University Professional Association for Human Resources. 2000-*01 Mid-Level Administrative/Professional Salary Survey*. Washington, D.C.: CUPA-HR.

This survey features median salary data from 1,135 public and private institutions on 134 positions, including reference specialist, cataloging specialist, Webmaster and other technology based positions. Data are organized by operating budget size and include regional comparisons. $130 for association members/survey participants, $180 for members/non-participants, $220 for nonmembers/survey non-participants. See contact information above.

Public Libraries

American Library Association. Public Library Association. *Public Library Data Service Statistical Report*. Chicago, IL: PLA.

Annual listing with information that includes library-specific salaries for directors and beginning librarians for most public libraries serving 100,000 or more and for many smaller libraries, as well as basic library statistics. The 2001 edition is available from ALA Customer Services Dept., 155 N. Wacker Dr., Chicago, IL 60606-1719, 800/545-2433, press 7, for $80 with the usual discounts for PLA and ALA members (ISBN 0-8389-8135-6).

Evelina R. Moulder. "Salaries of Municipal Officials, 2000" in *The Municipal Year Book,* 2001. Washington, D.C.: International City/County Management Association.

Chief librarian salaries for local public libraries are included with earnings of other city department heads. These are reported by geographic region, population size, city type (i.e., central, suburban, independent) and form of government. The mean, median, and first and third quartiles are included for libraries serving ten different population groups ranging from under 2,500 to over 1,000,000. *The Municipal Year Book* is published in April of each year and includes salary data from the previous year. To order, call 800-745-8780.

Sandstedt, Carl R. *Salary Survey: West-North-Central States.* St. Peters, Mo.: St. Charles City-County Library.

>This annual survey provides data for directors, assistant directors, department heads, starting MLS, and several support positions for public libraries in West-North-Central States (North Dakota, South Dakota, Nebraska, Kansas, Minnesota, Iowa, Missouri). Average salaries are presented by size of library budget. Also includes per FTE costs, per capita support, and per capita materials budget.
>
>St. Charles City-County Library, 425 Spencer Rd., Box 529, St. Peters, MO 63376, 636/441-2300, www.win.org/library/.

School Libraries

Educational Research Service. *Salaries and Wages for Professional and Support Personnel in Public Schools*, Arlington, VA: ERS, 2000-01.

>ERS publishes an annual report of salaries for public school personnel, which includes data for school librarians and library clerks. The report covers scheduled salaries for professional personnel and actual salaries paid for professional and support personnel by enrollment group, per pupil expenditure, and geographic region. It also includes year-to-year, five-year, and ten-year information on trends in public school salaries and wages, with comparisons to the Consumer Price Index for each of these periods. The report costs $150 (call for subscriber prices). Available from ERS, 2000 Clarendon Blvd., Arlington, VA 22201, 703/243-2100.

Marilyn L. Miller and Marilyn L. Shontz. "Expenditures for Resources in School Library Media Centers." *School Library Journal*.

>As part of a report every two years on budgets for and expenditures by school library media centers, some median and mean salary data for media specialists are reported by level of school. Included are comparisons of schools with and without district level library media coordinators. *School Library Journal*, 245 W. 17th St., New York, NY 10011, 212/463-6759, www.slj.com.

National Education Association. *Rankings and Estimates of School Statistics.* Washington, D.C.: NEA, 2000-01.

>Annual statistical data for the 50 states and District of Columbia includes rankings of school statistics, estimated average annual salaries of total instructional staff and also separate data for classroom teachers by state and region. Librarian data are not given separately, however, but are grouped with teachers, principals, supervisors, guidance and psychological personnel and related instructional workers.

For further information, contact NEA Professional Library, PO Box 2035, Annapolis Junction, MD 20701-2035, 800-229-4200, fax 301/206-9789, www.nea.org.

Specialized Libraries

American Association of Law Libraries. *Biennial Salary Survey 2001*. Chicago, IL: AALL.

The report summarizes salary information for law libraries with three following sections that cover academic libraries, private firm/corporate libraries and state, court and county libraries. The data is broken out and crossed-tabbed by position, region, gender, education, years in current position and years of library experience and further by geographical regions in the U.S.

The price for the publication is $95 for AALL members, $150 for nonmembers (includes shipping). Contact AALL, 53 W. Jackson Blvd., Suite 940, Chicago, IL 60604, 312/939-4764, fax 312/431-1097, www.aallnet.org. (AALL members may browse the online edition free of charge.)

Association of Academic Health Sciences Library Directors. *Annual Statistics of Medical School Libraries in the United States and Canada*. Seattle, WA: AAHSLD, 2000-01.

Salaries are provided for director, associate director, division head, department head, other librarians, and entry level positions. Minimum, maximum and mean are provided for the positions and arranged by region.

It is available at a cost of $20 for members of the Association of Academic Health Sciences Library Directors and $250 for nonmembers. The current edition and previous editions may be ordered by contacting AAHSLD, 2150 N. 107th St., #205, Seattle, WA 98133, 206/367-8704, fax 206/367-8777, www.aahsl.org.

Medical Library Association. *Health Sciences Librarian Compensation: Results of MLA's 1998 Salary Survey*. Chicago: MLA, 1998.

More than 1,900 members provided data for the 1998 triennial salary survey, available in summary format to MLA's members via the association's website, www.mlanet.org. The summary offers detailed information by job title, geographical area, type of institution, and more. Contact Kate Corcoran, MLA, 65 E. Wacker Pl., Suite 1900, Chicago, IL 60601-7298, 312/419-9094, ext. 12, www.mlanet.org.

Special Libraries Association. *SLA Annual Salary Survey*. Washington, D.C.: SLA, 2001.

Salaries are reported at the 25th, 50th (median) and 75th percentiles and contain breakdowns by industry, geographic region, administrative responsibility, sex, education level, and experience.

Data for the U.S. and Canada are presented in separate tables.

The Salary Survey is a comprehensive report containing the most accurate U.S. and Canadian salary information gathered by a member survey. A wide variety of variables are covered including industry type, geographical area, job title, budget range and years of experience.

The report, available in late fall to SLA members for $45, $54 non-members. Contact Marlena Hawkins, Special Libraries Association, 1700 18th St., N.W., Washington, D.C. 20009-2514, 202/939-3673, fax 202/265-9317, www.sla.org.

Other

Association for Library and Information Science Education. *ALISE Statistical Report and Database.* Reston, VA: ALISE, 1980-.

Average and median salaries for faculty and administrators in 56 ALISE member schools are provided in this annual report by sex, rank and term of appointment.

Back issues (1981-) of the report are available from ALISE, 11250 Roger Bacon Dr., #8, Reston, VA 20190-5202, 703/234-4146, fax 703/435-4390, alise@drohanmgmt.com, www.alise.org. Current issue is $65.00 (non-members), including postage and handling (U.S. funds), $35.00 for members. Annual report usually published in the summer.

College and University Professional Association for Human Resources. 2000-*01 National Faculty Salary Survey by Discipline and Rank in Private Four-Year Colleges and Universities.* Washington, D.C.: CUPA-HR.

College and University Professional Association for Human Resources. 2000-*01 National Faculty Salary Survey by Discipline and Rank in Public Four-Year Colleges and Universities.* Washington, D.C.: CUPA-HR.

Annual surveys collect data for five faculty ranks in 80 disciplines and major fields. A total of 531 private and 366 public institutions participated in the most recent study. Communications, Communication Technologies, Computer Information Sciences, and Library Sciences are included. The listings are for those who teach in library science programs, not those who hold faculty rank as academic librarians. Faculty Salary Surveys are each $80 for survey participants, $105 non-participant, CUPA-HR members; and $130 for non-participants, nonmembers from CUPA-HR, 1233 20th St., NW, Suite 301, Washington, D.C. 20036-1250, 202/429-0311, fax 202/429-0149, www.cupahr.org.

Gregory, Vicki L. "Placements and Salaries." *Library Journal.*

Annual survey since 1951 of ALA-accredited library and information studies education programs (usually published in the fall issue of *Library Journal* with data from previous calendar year.) For each reporting school, the low, high, average and median salaries are reported for men, women, and total placements. This information is also provided for five regions of the U.S. An additional table shows the distribution of high, low, average and median salaries by type of library for men, women and total placements. The latest listing, "Placements and Salaries 1999" was published in *Library Journal*, October 15, 2000.

Employee Benefits

Although some states collect data on employee benefits, little information is collected on a regional or national level on a regular basis for library workers.

PROVIDENCE Associates, Inc. *Public Library Work Benefits Survey*. Denton, TX: 1997.

> Results of a survey of 25 public libraries in 1997 provides salary ranges and average salaries for 5 staff levels, plus data on vacation days, sick leave, leave of absence, pension plans, health and life insurance, and other benefits. Single copies available for $10.00 plus $2.50 shipping/handling, from PROVIDENCE Associates, Inc., 488 Mill Dr., Second Floor, Cottonwood, AZ 86326-5340, 520/639-2798, fax 940/898-0201; aneyeforit@sedona.net. Look for the next survey in 2002.

Salary Surveys for Other Library Workers and Related Information Professionals

For salary data on other types of workers that may be employed in libraries, the following surveys might be useful:

Abbott, Langer and Associates, Inc., Dept NET, 548 First St., Crete, IL 60417, 708/672-4200, www.abbott-langer.com. Conducts annual or biennial salary surveys for the following fields: legal and related jobs in business and industry; industrial engineers; plant and facilities managers and engineers; consulting engineering firms; consulting firms; independent lab/testing/inspection firms; geologists; human resources/personnel department; service department; nonprofit organizations; research and development; manufacturing; food and beverage processing; security/loss prevention dept.; MIS/data processing; accounting departments; accounting firms; advertising agencies; sales/marketing management; direct marketing; life sciences and telecommunications.

> *Compensation in Nonprofit Organizations* contains information on salaries of Directors of Information with this type of employer. Mean, median, first and third quartile, and first and ninth decile data, salary ranges, current salaries, and total compensation (salaries plus bonuses) are reported by supervisory responsibility, type of nonprofit organization, total annual budget, geographic scope of organization, number of employees, region, state, and metropolitan area, and type of organization vs. remaining variables.

> *Available Pay Survey Reports: An Annotated Bibliography* (5th ed.) by Dr. Steven Langer (1999) contains annotations of over 1,200 salary surveys, both domestic and foreign. Annotations are indexed by source, geographic area, type of employer, and job title/function/college curricula.

The *Library Mosaics*, a bi-monthly magazine for support staff in libraries, media and information centers has published the "Library Support Staff Salary Survey" by Charlie Fox and Raymond Roney in the July/August 2000 issue. It provides a general overview of support staff, 310/645-4998.

The AMS Foundation Business Survey Group, PO Box 26644, Milwaukee, WI 53226, 800/229-5655. Conducts surveys of office/clerical, secretarial/administrative, professional, data processing and middle management jobs as well as pertinent business trends. The 2000 edition of the *Office/Clerical, Secretarial/Administrative, Professional, Data Processing and Management Survey* sells for $395. *Business Expenses and New Benefits, Contract Labor, Flexible Work, Internet Usage, Telecommuting, Training and Relocation*, and *Travel Expenses* sell for $30 each.

Datamation publishes an annual salary survey of computer and information systems personnel. The magazine reports on average salaries for positions in systems analysis, programming, database administration, data entry, office automation, and computer operations, by industry and regions. Results are based on averages or totals from the following information: salary, job type, job skills, and location, http://datamation.earthweb.com/.

U.S. Department of Labor, Bureau of Labor Statistics, National Compensation Survey program produces information on wages by occupation for many metroplitan areas and also for the nation as a whole. It provides data on occupational earnings, employer costs for wages, salaries, and benefits, and details of employer-provided benefit and establishment practices. This umbrella program combines the Occupational Compensation Surveys, the Employment Cost Index, and the Employee Benefits Survey and is published annually. For further information see http://stats.bls.gov/comhome.htm.

Appendix B

ALA Policies Relating to Salary Issues

The following are policies endorsed by the ALA Council and included in the "ALA Policy Manual" which appears annually in the *ALA Handbook of Organization*.

Policy #54.1 Library Education and Personnel Utilization

Sec. 8 The title "Librarian" carries with it the connotation of "professional" in the sense that professional tasks are those which require a special background and education on the basis of which library needs are identified, problems are analyzed, goals are set, and original and creative solutions are formulated for them, integrating theory into practice, and planning, organizing, communicating, and administering successful programs of service to users of the library's materials and services. In defining services to users, the professional person recognizes potential users as well as current ones, and designs services which will reach all who could benefit from them.

Sec. 9 The title "Librarian" therefore should be used only to designate positions in libraries which utilize the qualifications and impose the responsibilities suggested above. Positions which are primarily devoted to the routine application of established rules and techniques, however useful and essential to the effective operation of a library's ongoing services, should not carry the word "Librarian" in the job title.

Sec. 11 The salaries for each (personnel) category should offer a range of promotional steps sufficient to permit a career-in-rank. The top salary in any category should overlap the beginning salary in the next higher category, in order to give recognition to the value of experience and knowledge gained on the job.

Sec. 19 Administrative responsibilities entail advanced knowledge and skills comparable to those represented by any other high-level specialty, and appointment to positions in top administration should normally require the qualifications of a Senior Librarian with a specialization in administration. This category, however, is not limited to administrators, whose specialty is only one of several specializations of value to the library service. There are many areas of special knowledge within librarianship which are equally important and to which equal recognition in prestige and salary should be given. Highly qualified persons with specialist responsibilities in some aspects of librarianship--archives, bibliography, reference, for example--should be eligible for advanced status and financial rewards without being forced to abandon for administrative responsibilities their areas of major competence.

Policy #54.4 Comparable Rewards

The American Library Association supports salary administration which gives reasonable and comparable recognition to positions having administrative, technical, subject, and linguistic requirements. It is recognized that all such specialist competencies can be intellectually vigorous and meet demanding professional operational needs. In administering such a policy, it can be a useful guide that, in major libraries, as many nonadministrative specialties be assigned to the top classifications as are administrative staff. Whenever possible there should be as many at the top rank with less than 30 percent administrative load as there are at the highest rank carrying over 70 percent administrative load.

Policy #54.7 Security of Employment for Library Employees

Security of employment, as an elementary right, guarantees specifically.....a sufficient degree of economic security to make employment in the library attractive to men and women of ability.

Policy #54.8 The Library's Pay Plan

Libraries should have a well-constructed and well-administered pay plan based on systematic analysis and evaluation of jobs in the library and which will assure equal pay for equal work. (Note: For text of full statement, see section following listing of policies.)

Policy #54.9 Permanent Part-Time Employment

The right to earn a living includes a right to part-time employment on a par with full-time employment, including prorated pay and fringe benefits, opportunity for advancement and protection of tenure, access to middle and upper level jobs, and exercise of full responsibilities at any level.

ALA shall create more voluntarily chosen upgraded permanent part-time jobs in its own organization and supports similar action on the part of all libraries.

Policy #54.10 Equal Opportunity and Salaries

The American Library Association supports and works for the achievement of equal salaries and opportunity for employment and promotion for men and women.

The Association fully supports the concept of comparable wages for comparable work that aims at levels of pay for female-oriented occupations equal to those of male-oriented occupations; ALA therefore supports all legal and legislative efforts to achieve wages for library workers commensurate with wages in other occupations with similar qualifications, training, and responsibilities.

ALA particularly supports the efforts of those library workers who have documented, and are legally challenging, the practice of discriminatory salaries, and whose success will benefit all library workers throughout the nation.

Policy #54.11 Collective Bargaining

The American Library Association recognizes the principle of collective bargaining as one of the methods of conducting labor-management relations used by private and public institutions. The Association affirms the right of eligible library employees to organize and bargain collectively with their employers, or to refrain from organizing and bargaining collectively, without fear of reprisal.

Policy #54.18 Advertising Salary Ranges

Available ranges shall be given for positions listed in any placement services provided by ALA and its units. A regional salary guide delineating the latest minimum salary figures recommended by state library associations shall be made available from any placement services provided by ALA and its units.
    All ALA and unit publications printing classified job advertisements shall list the salary ranges established for open positions where available and shall include a regional salary guide delineating the latest minimum salary figures recommended by state library associations for library positions.

Full Text of Policy # 54.8: The Library's Pay Plan*

The American Library Association believes that an important factor in establishing and maintaining good library service is adequate pay for library employees as exemplified in a well-constructed and well-administered pay plan. A knowledge of the principles on which sound salary administration is based must be the foundation of an equitable pay plan. To aid the library's governing board, its administration, and its staff in the formulation, promulgation, and operation of such a pay plan, the ALA Board on Personnel Administration sets forth in a series of related statements the principles of salary planning and administration.

1. A sound pay plan will be predicated on a systematic analysis and evaluation of jobs in the library, and will reflect the current organization and objectives of the library, recognizing different levels of difficulty and responsibility inherent in various positions, whether these are classified as professional, nonprofessional, administrative, specialist, maintenance, or trade; the relationship among positions in terms of difficulty and responsibility will thus be expressed in a unified plan which will integrate all types of service and will assure equal pay for equal work.

2. An equitable salary schedule will be provided for each class of position which is comparable to that received by persons employed in analogous work in the area and required to have analogous training and qualifications.

The salaries of nonprofessional employees, maintenance and skilled trade workers employed by the library system will compare with those of local workers performing similar duties. The salary schedules for professional library positions, in the case of the community where the pay scale does not meet competing rates outside, may need to exceed the prevailing local level for other professional personnel. Since the recruiting of professionally trained librarians is on a nation-wide basis, the library system must compete with rates paid in the country as a whole in order to obtain and retain a high quality of professional personnel. In libraries in educational institutions (elementary, secondary, and higher education) the professional librarians will normally be on the faculty pay plan, with the salary schedules of the various classes of faculty rank adjusted to compensate equitably for such factors as shorter vacations and longer work week; where a separate pay plan is used, it will be comparable with that of the faculty and adjusted to compensate equitably for such factors as vacation and work week.

3. An equitable salary schedule will provide for each class of position a minimum and a maximum salary and a series of increments within each salary range, such increments to be granted on the basis of demonstrated competence, individual development (whether through growth on the job or through formal education), and attitude.

*Note: This policy was passed by the ALA Council in July 1955. It still remains a useful statement regarding the administration of a library's pay plan. Readers should note, however, that the references to the Board on Personnel Administration are not applicable since this unit is no longer in existence

4. The library system in developing a pay plan, and in reviewing it to maintain its adequacy, will identify one or more key positions in the professional and in the other services, set salary schedules for these positions which are comparable to prevailing rates for such positions, and develop and adjust the salary schedule for other levels of positions in relation to the salary schedules set for each of these key positions.

5. The pay plan ladder consisting of the salary schedules for the various classes of positions will provide an orderly progression from the lowest to the highest schedule, with each schedule reflecting properly the difference in level of duties and responsibilities of positions in that classification from those in the schedule below and above it but without wide gaps or serious overlapping between schedules.

6. An equitable pay plan will reflect living costs in the community, the cost of maintaining an appropriate level of living, and the ability of the jurisdiction to pay for the service.

7. All policies and rules concerning the operation and administration of the pay plan will be set forth clearly in writing and will accompany the pay plan.

8. Though final approval and adoption of the pay plan and rules for its operation rest with the governing board and administration of the library, it is desirable that the library staff participates in the formulation of both the plan and its operating rules.

9. Each staff member will be informed of the salary schedule for his or her class of position, of the relation of that schedule to the pay plan as a whole, and of the policies and rules governing the operation of the plan.

The current studies of the ALA Board on Personnel Administration giving salary data for key positions will provide useful material for the library system in developing and maintaining the adequacy of its pay plan.

Appendix C

Technical Considerations

Formation of Library Groups

As in previous years, the survey samples were selected from two library universes – public and academic. The public library universe included all public libraries serving populations of 25,000 or more and was stratified into two classes – those serving populations of from 25,000 to 99,999 and those serving populations of 100,000 or more.

The academic library universe was stratified into three categories: two-year college, four-year college, and university using the 1998 Academic Library Survey file. This file includes codes for the categories created by the Carnegie Foundation for the Advancement of Teaching in 1994. Our "two-year college" corresponds to the Carnegie category "Associate of Arts." Our "four-year college" category corresponds to the Carnegie Categories "Baccalaureate I and II." Our "university" includes the Carnegie categories "Master's I and II, Doctoral I and II, and Research I and II."

Within each of these five strata, libraries were furthered stratified into four geographic areas used frequently by National Center for Education Statistics (NCES): North Atlantic, Great Lakes and Plains, Southeast, West, and Southwest. A list of states included in each region is provided in Table D-1. As in previous surveys, the five library classes and four geographic areas were combined to form twenty groups from which samples were selected. Tables D2-D7 show the size of each group, the size of the sample, and the size of the return.

Sample Selection and Return

The size of the sample for each type/size/geographic strata was determined by using a proportional sampling procedure that took into account the size of the population in each group and the expected return rate for the survey. The public library sample was selected using a file from the NCES containing 1998 data on all public libraries submitted to NCES by state library agencies as part of the Federal State Cooperative System for Public Library Data (FSCS). This file includes data on the number of staff with master's degrees from programs in library and information studies accredited by ALA. Before selecting the sample, we dropped from the sampling frame libraries that did not have at least two of such personnel and libraries that had refused to respond in the years from 1990 through 2000 for reasons that seemed unlikely to change.

The procedure for selecting the academic library sample was similar to the procedure followed in previous years. The Library Research Center (LRC) created a sampling frame by using the universe file described above (see second paragraph) and screening out several sets of institutions. Removed were institutions with fewer than two full-time professionals and institutions categorized as "specialized" by the Carnegie Corporation for the Advancement of Teaching. Those institutions offer degrees ranging from the bachelor's to the doctorate, at least 50 percent of which are in a single specialized field, e.g., "theological seminaries, Bible colleges, and other institutions offering degrees in religion," and "Schools of art, music, and design." Specialized institutions often declined to respond in the early years of this survey. Also excluded were four sets of institutions whose individual members had been unable to respond in the past. In New York, the seventeen institutions that are part of the City University of New York were removed because librarians there have full academic status and salary is not related to position description. Public two-year schools in California were removed for the same reason as were the fourteen members of the state university system in Pennsylvania. Also in Pennsylvania, we removed all but the main campus of Pennsylvania State University because librarians at other campuses declined to respond in the past and referred us to the main campus.

Finally we removed libraries that had refused to respond in the years from 1990 through 2000 for reasons that seemed unlikely to change. The remaining institutions were sampled using the stratification plan described above.

In addition to the 931 returns analyzed for this report, we also received 16 returns that could not be used. They fell into the following categories:

- one was from a library where none of the staff are full-time or none of the full-time staff had master's degrees from programs in library and information studies accredited by ALA.

- twelve refused for various reasons. Six of these were from academic libraries where salary data are confidential by institutional policy. Two were from an academic libraries where a search for Director was in progress. The other four gave various reasons for refusal.

- three were from academic institutions that did not have a library or had a joint library with another college.

Procedure

The questionnaire and cover letter were mailed on April 12, 2001. A postage-paid business reply envelope was enclosed to encourage response. A second mailing was sent to all non-respondents in May. A third mailing was sent in June only to non-respondents in several strata where response was under 70 percent. Questionnaires were returned to the Library Research Center (LRC) of the University of Illinois Graduate School of Library and Information Science, where they were coded, entered into a data file, cleaned, and analyzed using SPSS for Windows.

Again this year a special procedure was followed for libraries that are members of the Association of Research Libraries (ARL). ARL, which includes about 100 of the largest university libraries in the U.S., conducts its own annual salary survey. Data are gathered for salaries as of July 1 and published the following spring. ARL libraries are also included in the sample for the ALA survey. In the past, some have declined to answer because they are unable to spend time completing another salary questionnaire. For the 2001 survey, ARL again agreed to cooperate with us to save work for everyone. After the sample was selected, we identified the ARL libraries on the list and sent the directors a special mailing asking them to release salaries already on file with ARL. Twenty-two of the twenty-six ARL libraries in the sample agreed to release data. We sent ARL a list of the ARL position codes that matched the position descriptions in our questionnaire and ARL sent salary data to LRC electronically for those positions in the selected institutions. These salaries were entered into the data file along with salaries reported on the questionnaire.

This procedure worked well and saved time both in the libraries involved and in survey processing. It has two drawbacks, however. ARL does not specify that salaries should be reported only for staff with master's degrees from programs in library and information studies accredited by ALA and some ARL libraries include "other professionals" as well as librarians. For the most part, however, we expect that those "other professionals" are in the ARL position code of "Functional Specialist" which was *not* on the list of codes we requested from ARL. Also, the ARL survey does not ask respondents to indicate the type of staff supervised which is the key distinction between two categories in the ALA survey: Department Heads/Coordinators/Senior Managers and Managers/Supervisors of Support Staff. Because we are aware of the burden it will place on ARL libraries to ask them to complete the new questionnaire, we decided to use as much data as we could from ARL and accept the fact that salaries at ARL libraries are not included for the two positions just noted.

Table C-1. States in Four Regions of the U.S.

North Atlantic	Great Lakes and Plains	Southeast	West and Southwest
Connecticut	Illinois	Alabama	Alaska
Delaware	Indiana	Arkansas	Arizona
District of Columbia	Iowa	Florida	California
Maine	Kansas	Georgia	Colorado
Maryland	Michigan	Kentucky	Hawaii
Massachusetts	Minnesota	Louisiana	Idaho
New Hampshire	Missouri	Mississippi	Montana
New Jersey	Nebraska	North Carolina	Nevada
New York	North Dakota	South Carolina	New Mexico
Pennsylvania	Ohio	Tennessee	Oklahoma
Rhode Island	South Dakota	Virginia	Oregon
Vermont	Wisconsin	West Virginia	Texas
			Utah
			Washington
			Wyoming

SOURCE: STATISITCS OF PUBLIC LIBRARIES, 1977-1978 (NCES, 1982)

Table C-2. Medium-Sized Public Libraries: Size of Group, Sample, Return

	GROUP	SAMPLE		RETURN	
	#	#	% of Group	#	% of Sample
North Atlantic	322	123	38.2	86	69.9
Great Lakes and Plains	318	121	38.1	89	73.6
Southeast	183	70	38.3	46	65.7
West and Southwest	188	72	38.3	56	77.8
TOTAL	1,011	386	38.2	277	71.8

Table C-3. Large Public Libraries: Size of Group, Sample, Return

	GROUP	SAMPLE		RETURN	
	#	#	% of Group	#	% of Sample
North Atlantic	65	46	70.8	31	67.4
Great Lakes and Plains	91	46	50.5	38	82.6
Southeast	131	60	45.8	41	68.3
West and Southwest	159	82	51.6	62	75.6
TOTAL	446	234	52.5	172	73.5

Table C-4. Two-Year College Libraries: Size of Group, Sample, Return

	GROUP	SAMPLE		RETURN	
	#	#	% of Group	#	% of Sample
North Atlantic	134	46	34.3	26	56.5
Great Lakes and Plains	135	46	34.1	32	69.6
Southeast	208	66	31.7	33	50.0
West and Southwest	154	49	31.8	28	57.1
TOTAL	631	207	32.8	119	57.5

Table C-5. Four-Year College Libraries: Size of Group, Sample, Return

	GROUP	SAMPLE		RETURN	
	#	#	% of Group	#	% of Sample
North Atlantic	85	45	52.9	23	51.1
Great Lakes and Plains	90	46	51.1	29	63.0
Southeast	95	46	48.4	22	47.8
West and Southwest	26	26	100.0	15	57.7
TOTAL	296	163	55.1	89	54.6

Table C-6. University Libraries: Size of Group, Sample, Return

	GROUP	SAMPLE		RETURN	
	#	#	% of Group	#	% of Sample
North Atlantic	269	85	31.6	52	61.2
Great Lakes and Plains	252	79	31.3	56	70.9
Southeast	233	73	31.3	49	67.1
West and Southwest	223	70	31.4	52	74.3
TOTAL	977	307	31.4	209	68.1

Table C-7. All Libraries Surveyed: Size of Group, Sample, Return

	GROUP	SAMPLE		RETURN	
	#	#	% of Group	#	% of Sample
North Atlantic	875	345	39.4	218	63.2
Great Lakes and Plains	886	338	38.1	244	72.2
Southeast	850	315	37.1	191	60.6
West and Southwest	750	299	39.9	213	71.2
TOTAL	3,361	1,297	38.6	866	66.8

Appendix D

American Library Association
50 East Huron Street
Chicago, Illinois 60611-2795
USA

Telephone 312 944 6780
Fax 312 440 9374
Toll Free 800 545 2433
TDD 312 944 7298
E-mail: ala@ala.org
http://www.ala.org

ALAAmerican Library Association

April 12, 2001

Dear Colleague:

ALA needs your help in providing information to the library community. The enclosed survey concerns salaries paid to librarians with master's degrees from programs in library and information studies accredited by ALA who hold full-time positions in academic and public libraries. Your institution has been selected as part of a random sample of libraries to receive the enclosed questionnaire. Only summary results will be reported; individual responses will not be identified.

ALA collected and published similar information biennially from 1982 to 1988, and annually since 1989. The results of these surveys have been useful to librarians applying for positions, to librarians setting salaries, and to many others interested in the compensation of librarians. If you have completed this survey before, please note that the categories are somewhat different. Beginning with the 1999 survey, the categories focus on the nature of responsibility for the work of other staff.

Because your library is one of a scientifically selected sample, your response is essential to the success of the survey. As an indication of our thanks for your help, all participants are entitled to a 25% discount on the price of the report. (Mention this entitlement when you place an order. The report will be published in September, 2001.) If your staff is very large and this form is difficult to use, please contact Mary Jo Lynch using one of the methods given below. We want your response and will work with you to make use of whatever data you can provide.

Please complete the questionnaire and return it in the enclosed self-addressed, postage-paid envelope. Please return it as soon as possible, but no later than May 4, 2001. If you have questions about the survey, please contact Mary Jo Lynch, Director, ALA Office for Research and Statistics at 1-800-545-2433, ext. 1-4273 or mlynch@ala.org.

Thank you very much for your cooperation.

Sincerely yours,

William R. Gordon
Executive Director
American Library Association

WRG/jmg

P.S. In order to ensure the validity of the survey results, reminders will be sent to nonrespondents. However, we would rather spend the postage money on other services. Please help our budget by returning this form promptly.

Appendix E

AMERICAN LIBRARY ASSOCIATION

SURVEY OF LIBRARIAN SALARIES, 2001

- This survey requests annual salaries paid to full-time professional librarians, i.e., persons who have master's degrees from programs in library and information studies accredited by the ALA.

- It is our expectation that each full-time professional librarian on your library's staff will fit into one of the six categories on this survey. Therefore, salaries for all full-time professional librarians should be reported.

- Please report the actual salary paid to each full-time person in the categories below as of April 1, 2001. Do not include benefits.

- If it is easier for you to use separate sheets of paper or attach a computer printout, please feel free to do so. Also, if you have more employees than the number of spaces provided in a given section, please list additional salaries on a separate piece of paper, and label it with the appropriate category from the survey form.

- If two or more persons in a category have the same annual salary, you need not write the salary more than once. **Instead** indicate the number of persons receiving the particular amount. (e.g., 2@$37,500).

SPECIAL NOTE FOR ACADEMIC LIBRARIES:

- If an incumbent is considered full-time but works LESS than a 12-month year (including vacation), please report the salary and circle the appropriate number of months (9 or 10) for which the salary is paid. The numbers are on the form to the right of each salary line.

- If services are contributed (i.e., institution pays some expenses or an honorarium but not a true salary), please do not list the incumbent.

PART I. SALARIES PAID TO BEGINNING LIBRARIANS

In the last six months did you hire, for full-time work, one or more persons who have master's degrees from programs in library and information studies accredited by ALA but no professional experience after receiving the degree?

           Yes   1 (PLEASE LIST ANNUAL SALARIES BELOW)

           No   2 (PLEASE CONTINUE THE SURVEY)

```
           9                  9                  9                  9
1_____10        3_____10        5_____10        7_____10

           9                  9                  9                  9
2_____10        4_____10        6_____10        8_____10
```

Note: Do not repeat these salaries elsewhere on this form.

PART II. SALARIES PAID TO EXPERIENCED LIBRARIANS

Director/Dean*:

List salary of chief officer of the library or library system.

```
                     9
Annual Salary_____10
```

Deputy/Associate/Assistant Director* :

List annual salaries of persons who report to the Director and manage major aspects of the library operation (e.g., technical services, public services, collection development, systems/automation).

1_____9_10   3_____9_10   5_____9_10   7_____9_10

2_____9_10   4_____9_10   6_____9_10   8_____9_10

Department Heads/Coordinators/Senior Managers*:

List annual salaries of persons who supervise one or more professional librarians*.

1_____9_10   6_____9_10   11_____9_10   16_____9_10

2_____9_10   7_____9_10   12_____9_10   17_____9_10

3_____9_10   8_____9_10   13_____9_10   18_____9_10

4_____9_10   9_____9_10   14_____9_10   19_____9_10

5_____9_10   10_____9_10   15_____9_10   20_____9_10

Managers/Supervisors of support staff*:

List annual salaries of persons who supervise support staff in any part of the library but do <u>not</u> supervise professional librarians.

1_____9_10   5_____9_10   9_____9_10   13_____9_10

2_____9_10   6_____9_10   10_____9_10   14_____9_10

3_____9_10   7_____9_10   11_____9_10   15_____9_10

4_____9_10   8_____9_10   12_____9_10   16_____9_10

* Report only full-time staff *with master's degrees from programs in library and information studies accredited by ALA*. Do not repeat salaries from Part 1.

Librarians who do not supervise:

List annual salaries of full-time staff with master's degrees from programs in library and information studies accredited by ALA who were not reported earlier and who have no supervisory responsibilities.

1 _____ 9/10	7 _____ 9/10	13 _____ 9/10	19 _____ 9/10
2 _____ 9/10	8 _____ 9/10	14 _____ 9/10	20 _____ 9/10
3 _____ 9/10	9 _____ 9/10	15 _____ 9/10	21 _____ 9/10
4 _____ 9/10	10 _____ 9/10	16 _____ 9/10	22 _____ 9/10
5 _____ 9/10	11 _____ 9/10	17 _____ 9/10	23 _____ 9/10
6 _____ 9/10	12 _____ 9/10	18 _____ 9/10	24 _____ 9/10

PART III. SUPPLEMENTARY QUESTIONS

Experts on human resources write and speak about the importance of staff development and training in maintaining a productive workforce. Articles on this topic often refer to studies that report expenditures for staff development and training as a percent of payroll in a particular industry. Your answers to the following questions will give us data on that topic for the library workforce.

1. What was your total payroll in the most recently completed fiscal year? Include salaries and wages for all staff. Do not include benefits.

   Total Payroll $_____

2. Estimate your direct costs for staff development and training for all staff in the most recently completed fiscal year. This might include: expenditures for development and delivery of formal education events on site (e.g., speaker fees, materials), travel costs and registration fees for conferences, institutes, seminars, workshops, classes held off site, distance education, job related tuition reimbursement, purchase or rental of training materials (e.g., video, software), cost of a staff development office.

   Direct cost of staff development and training $_____

PLEASE CONTINUE

Name and title of respondent*: _____

_____

Telephone number: _____

Fax number: _____

E-mail address: _____

* Neither libraries nor individuals will be identified in the report of this survey. The name of your library is given on the last page so that we can avoid sending reminders to libraries who respond. The name, phone, fax, and email address of the person responding are requested because we may need to contact him or her if we have questions about this return.

THANK YOU VERY MUCH! *Please return by May 4, 2001 in the enclosed postage paid envelope.* If you lose the reply envelope, please send the form to:

Library Research Center
University of Illinois at Urbana-Champaign
501 East Daniel Street
Champaign Illinois 61820

Appendix F

Salaries Paid for Less Than a Twelve Month Year in Academic Libraries

Instructions on the questionnaire told the respondent: If the incumbent works **less** than a 12-month year (including vacation), please report the salary and circle the appropriate number of months (9 or 10) for which the salary is paid. A program was written to prorate these salaries to their twelve month equivalents for the purpose of reporting results of this survey. Table G was created to show how often this process was necessary. The first column shows the total tables in this report. The second column shows how many were reported as being for nine months and the third column shows the percentage of incumbents in the category (position/type of library) which that number represents. The following columns repeat that pattern for positions reported as being for ten months and then for a combination of nine and ten month salaries.

Table G.

Salaries Paid for Less Than a 12-month Year in Academic Libraries							
POSITION AND TYPE OF LIBRARY	ALL INCUMBENTS #	9-MONTH #	%	10-MONTH* #	%	9 AND 10 MONTH #	%
Director							
Two-year college	106	3	3	3	3	6	6
Four-year college	85	0	0	5	6	5	6
University	203	0	0	1	<1	1	<1
Deputy/Associate/Assistant Directors							
Two-year college	57	7	12	4	7	11	19
Four-year college	69	1	1	3	4	4	6
University	304	2	<1	4	1	6	2
Department Heads/Coordinators/Senior Managers							
Two-year college	50	5	10	3	6	8	16
Four-year college	32	0	0	2	6	2	6
University	311	4	1	7	2	11	4
Managers/Supervisors of Support Staff							
Two-year college	89	13	15	13	15	26	29
Four-year college	126	2	2	6	5	8	6
University	521	3	<1	10	2	13	2
Librarians who do not supervise							
Two-year college	131	22	17	12	9	34	26
Four-year college	117	8	7	16	14	24	21
University	1,167	11	<1	38	3	49	4
Beginning Librarians							
Two-year college	12	2	17	0	0	2	19
Four-year college	22	1	5	1	5	2	9
University	71	2	3	3	4	5	7

* includes 28 11-month salaries